speed up!

A kinaesthetic programme to develop fluent handwriting

Lois Addy

Acknowledgements

Many thanks to Dr Christine Mayers and Anne Longmore, colleagues at York St John, College of the University of Leeds, for their helpful and constructive comments on the contents of this programme. Thank you also to Gemma and Imogen for kindly allowing me to use their handwriting samples.

Permission to photocopy

This book contains worksheets which may be reproduced by photocopier or other means for use by the purchaser. This permission is granted on the understanding that these copies will be used within the educational establishment of the purchaser. This book and all its contents remain copyright. Copies may be made without reference to the publisher or the licensing scheme for the making of photocopies operated by the Publishers Licensing Agency.

Speed Up!

LL01613

ISBN 1 85503 386 0

© Lois Addy

Illustrations © Robin Lawrie

All rights reserved

First published 2004

Reprinted 2004 (June)

The right of Lois Addy to be identified as author of this work has been asserted by her in accordance with sections 77 and 78 of the Copyright, Designs and Patents Act 1988.

Printed in the UK for LDA

Duke Street, Wisbech, Cambs, PE13 2AE UK

Contents

1 Introduction

Within a school day a child spends, on average, one third of their time on writing activities relating to language tasks, one quarter of their time on writing tasks relating to general studies including topic work, and a further, smaller proportion on writing related to mathematics. These were the findings based on 58 primary classrooms as part of Leicester University's Observations, Research and Classroom Learning Education project (ORACLE) (Galton; referred to in Graves, 1980). Despite the age of the study, this is true today. Charles Cripps, former tutor at the Cambridge Institute of Education and author of the handwriting scheme A Hand for Spelling, suggests that the majority of time children spend in the classroom is devoted to communication activities: listening, talking, reading and writing (Cripps, 2001). Of these four, writing takes up the greatest amount of time. Cripps suggests that children spend 55 per cent of their communication time involved in writing-related tasks in Key Stage 1, rising to 65 per cent in Key Stage 2.

In an average school day, a child spends over half of their time engaged in writing tasks of some kind. We might therefore assume that the mechanical process of handwriting would be well taught, so that all children would be able to write fluently, comfortably, quickly and legibly.

There are now many programmes that do an excellent job of guiding children through the early stages of handwriting development. The majority of these are focused on developing handwriting skills in Key Stage 1, with the assumption that by the age of 8 years, children will have mastered the basics of legible, fluent handwriting.

However, there are many children in Key Stage 2 who still struggle with handwriting, to the extent that it constitutes a very real hindrance to learning and achievement. The difficulty can become a source of concern and stress for the child, and of frustration for the teacher attempting to decipher illegible work.

Unfortunately, many teachers lack the resources, expertise and – perhaps most significantly – the time to tackle the problem. At Key Stage 3, difficulties with handwriting are compounded by the demands of the secondary system and children are even less likely to receive any specific help.

Speed Up! is a short but effective programme, designed for use with children from Year 3 to Year 8 (8–13 years) whose writing could be characterised as:

○ laboured;
○ slow;
○ illegible;
○ lacking fluency;
○ an uncomfortable mixture of print and cursive lettering.

These will include children whose difficulties are simply the result of developing handwriting habits that hinder fluency.

They will also include those who have a developmental coordination disorder, dyslexia or ADHD. The programme is effective with children with certain types of neurological impairment, such as diplegic cerebral palsy, but it is not suitable for young people with muscular dystrophy (Duchennes).

The programme may also be used with children older than 13 years who want to work on speed and fluency and are motivated to improve their handwriting.

The approach is completely different from the rehearsal and practice of letter forms and patterns used in traditional methods. Instead, the training focuses on movements to develop kinaesthetic awareness and sensitivity in order to improve handwriting fluency and speed. It does not teach correct letter formation, although the motor responses and orientation required for correct letter formation are fostered by the motor tasks.

Delivering the Speed Up! programme requires no special training and the sessions may be led by a teacher, therapist or teaching assistant.

The significance of handwriting problems

Many children in Year 3 and later have difficulties in joining letters appropriately, having struggled with the transition from print to cursive in Year 2. These struggles may be exacerbated from Year 4 onwards, when children are expected to be able to write in a fluent, cursive style and with increasing speed – all in anticipation of the requirements of the secondary education system.

During the secondary years, even greater emphasis is placed on increasing speed of output in order to accommodate note taking, homework, testing and, ultimately, examinations. In addition, writing speed and legibility need to be sustained over prolonged periods of time; speed often decreases as fatigue sets in, which can be a particular problem in examinations.

The development of fast, fluent handwriting does not always occur automatically. Many children at the point of transfer into secondary school do not possess the writing skills they need in order to cope with the demands of secondary education. This may be due to developmental delay, specific learning difficulty or neurological impairment. Or it may be simply that they have been allowed to write in an inappropriate way for prolonged periods without correction. Whatever the cause, the activity of handwriting for these children requires 'an inordinate amount of mental and physical energy' (Carter and Synolds, 1974;

The ability to produce legible handwriting at speed has been shown to make a significant contribution to achievement. Research reported in *The Times* (Charter, 2000) found that students who can write quickly can achieve up to a grade higher at GCSE, regardless of academic ability. The researchers concluded, 'continued attention to handwriting throughout the school years is essential and an early start with joined writing will aid a process that is far more than purely a physical activity'.

Schneck, 1991). As a result, they become despondent and reluctant to write.

How the Speed Up! programme was developed

The Speed Up! programme is the result of over 15 years' intensive research and practice by the author, who is a paediatric occupational therapist. The complex skill of handwriting was highlighted by parents and professionals as presenting a very particular challenge. Initial work was done with children under the age of 8 years; it was found that they responded well to selecting and grading activities which addressed perceptual and motor skills relating to writing. But when the activities were tried with older children, the improvements were not so encouraging.

Gradually, a programme was developed that would better address the problems experienced by children of 8 years and up. It was based largely on multisensory activities, including kinaesthetic games. The programme evolved over several years and was influenced by work in related fields. In particular, it drew from psycho-motor therapy, used to help children with motor coordination difficulties (Geddes, 1981; Kerr, 1982); from the work of Kirshner (1972), whose book *Training that Makes Sense* provided many kinaesthetic activity ideas; and from research by Laszlo and Bairstow (1984). Thus, the Speed Up! programme comprises an eclectic mix of kinaesthetic, psycho-motor and perceptual-motor activities.

Although the Speed Up! programme was originally developed as a resource for occupational therapists, this book is designed for use by teachers, teaching assistants and therapists. The programme is being continually evaluated in schools and child development centres across the UK.

How is the programme delivered?

The Speed Up! programme is:

- suitable for use with any child from Year 3 through to Year 8 (8–13 years);
- presented in eight weekly sessions lasting an hour or less;
- administered by a teacher or teaching assistant;
- done in small groups (three children is an ideal number);
- fun and enjoyable.

The programme begins with an assessment, which is easy to administer and takes only a few minutes. This assessment helps both the teacher and the pupil to be aware of any specific areas of difficulty and provides a baseline against which to measure progress.

Following initial assessment, the programme itself is delivered in eight weekly sessions of 45–60 minutes. The child is also required to practise at home between sessions. Ideally this practice should be done daily but a minimum of three times a week is necessary for the programme to be effective.

Sessions are organised with small groups of pupils who are experiencing similar difficulties. Groups of three are ideal. The programme may also be used with individual children, but some of the activities and games will need to be modified slightly. These activities can still be enjoyable and effective, especially if the trainer 'plays' as well.

The sessions incorporate a balance of rhythmic patterning, kinaesthetic exercises and perceptual challenges, all done in a relaxed way with the emphasis on fun.

After the weekly sessions the assessment is repeated.

Handwriting style

The Speed Up! programme is compatible with any handwriting style. The majority of primary schools in the UK teach a non-looped style, and the use of loops is not encouraged. The programme is effective with non-looped styles, but to gain maximum improvement a looped style is better. There is evidence that the use of 'speed loops' on ascenders and descenders improves not only fluency but also speed. This is because in non-looped writing, these not only require an extra pen lift but also leave the pen moving in the wrong direction (Roe, 1994).

There are many programmes which can help you adopt a looped style (for example *Loops and Other Groups* by Mary Benbow and *Write Dance* by Ragnhild Oussoren Voors). A complete Victorian modern cursive script model, commonly used in Australia, is available online.

However, it is acknowledged that not all teachers and pupils will want to adopt such a style, and models for both looped and non-looped styles are provided within the Speed Up! programme.

How to use this book

This book provides all you need to deliver the Speed Up! handwriting programme. Chapter 2 outlines briefly the development of handwriting and approaches to teaching the skill. By looking at the particular difficulties experienced by older children as well as the main causes of those difficulties, the reasons for using a kinaesthetic approach are made clear.

For those who are interested, Chapter 3 provides an overview of the theory behind the approach. A theoretical understanding of the physiology is by no means essential for successful delivery of the programme, but knowing a little about the principles involved may provide some useful insights as you work with pupils.

In Chapter 4 you will find full details of how to run the Speed Up! programme, beginning with the assessment. Clear instructions for each weekly session are provided on pages which may be photocopied; it may be helpful to make copies for use in the sessions, especially if a teaching assistant is acting as the trainer.

2

The development and teaching of handwriting

Handwriting is not an innate ability but a complex psycho-motor skill that requires instruction, experience and practice. *Hand*writing, by definition, is the graphic result of motor, perceptual and cognitive processes used to represent real objects and events, and later to represent the words of spoken language.

Despite the advances in technology which have given rise to word-processors, lap-top computers and voice recognition software, handwriting continues to have many uses in everyday life. Although the amount of handwriting produced by most adults is undoubtedly diminishing, we continue to write shopping lists, letters and cards, and reminder notes to ourselves.

More significantly, within our present education system handwriting is still the main medium through which evidence of learning is produced. Children are introduced to this complex fine-motor and perceptual skill in their Reception year and are expected to develop it over the course of the following years, becoming faster and more fluent with time and practice.

The teaching of handwriting

The teaching of handwriting begins with pre-writing patterns to develop fine-motor pencil control. Letter forms are then introduced, usually with their ligatures (connecting lines). Once writing in print has been established, usually in Year 2, children are taught how to join their letters to produce cursive writing.

National Curriculum criteria relating to handwriting state *what* a child is expected to achieve, but little guidance is given on *how* the child can be encouraged to achieve it. It is interesting that the National Curriculum offers no guidelines for handwriting from Year 5 onwards; presumably the assumption is that by the age of 10, children will have mastered the skill and will be able to write quickly, efficiently and legibly.

According to the National Literacy Strategy Framework, by the end of Year 3 it is expected that pupils should be able to do the following:

○ Build up handwriting speed.

○ Increase fluency and legibility.

○ Be proficient in the implementation of the four basic joins introduced in Year 2.

These include:

- diagonal joins to letters without ascenders, e.g. **ai**, **ar**, **un**;

- horizontal joins to letters without ascenders, e.g. **ou**, **vi**, **wi**;

- diagonal joins to letters with ascenders, e.g. **ab**, **ul**, **it**;

- horizontal joins to letters with ascenders, e.g. **ol**, **wh**, **ot**.

○ Ensure consistency in size and proportions of letters and the spacing between letters and words.

In order to achieve these goals, a child must have well-coordinated motor skills, intact visual perception and good kinaesthetic sense, and a sense of fluency and rhythm when writing.

Difficulties with handwriting

In order to develop fast, fluent handwriting, children need:

- refined kinaesthesia;
- efficient motor planning;
- accurate hand–eye coordination;
- intact visuo–motor integration;
- in-hand manipulation;
- to appreciate the rhythmic qualities of writing, knowing where and when to join according to letter form;
- to know where to position and lift the wrist;
- to comprehend word construction;
- to apply appropriate pressure through the writing instrument – too much will slow down the movement, too little will reduce fine-motor control;
- to organise the page spatially, knowing where to start, how to track across horizontally, and where to finish;
- to be able to write without viewing every letter and word in order to copy from books, black or white boards, and to take dictation.

If this looks like an impossibly advanced set of skills, remember that they have been acquired by all children who are able to produce fluent handwriting!

Nevertheless, there are many children who have not been able to acquire all of these skills. Many children also have difficulties in joining letters appropriately, having struggled with the transition from print to cursive in Year 2. These children may have spent the first two or three years of their school career producing acceptable, legible print, but find joining letters problematic. Difficulties will certainly arise if the child has been forming letters in reverse, for example writing the letter **o** by circling in a clockwise rather than an anticlockwise direction. Problems may also arise if the child is not sure about which letters to join and where; often these children will focus on 'drawing' letter shapes, rather than on creating whole words. They will tend to see writing as a series of letters in a sequence, rather than a series of whole-word units.

Handwriting difficulty from Year 3 onwards can be evidenced in many different ways. You may notice that the child:

- exerts heavy pressure through the writing instrument;
- exhibits signs of stress when writing;
- is unable to produce a volume of writing equal to that of their peers;
- complains of an aching wrist and hand cramps;
- has long pauses in the middle of writing tasks;
- is reluctant to write at all.

You may also find that the child's writing:

- lacks fluency;
- lacks rhythm;
- is laboured and slow;
- has words with joins and breaks between letters in the wrong places;
- has incorrectly joined letters;
- has erratic ascenders and descenders that go in odd directions.

In this sample it can be seen that some letters are very light and others dark. This is because Imogen struggles to apply appropriate pressure through the writing instrument. Many letters are incompletely formed, indicating a problem with form constancy which will affect how she joins letters. Writing alignment is very upright, which indicates that Imogen is holding her arm against her body when she writes. As a result, the writing appears cramped and this can affect legibility. Imogen is not completely comfortable when joining letters and easily returns to print, and as she does so spaces are omitted between words. Overall, her writing style lacks fluency; this is possibly the result of low muscle tone and a tight pencil grip.

> Baar-Baar Black sheep
> Have you any wool
> Yes sir, yes sir three Bags fool
> One for the marster
> one for the dame
> and one for the little boy
> who lives down the lane.
> Baar-Baar

Handwriting by Imogen, aged 9 years

There are a number of possible reasons for handwriting difficulties. The main ones are as follows:

- Incorrect orientation of letters at print stage leads to problems in joining when cursive script is required.
- Pressure to write faster may result in the child feeling physical tension and this may reduce motor confidence.

○ Poor kinaesthetic regulation may lead to increased pressure on the writing instrument.

○ A lack of rhythm in motor coordination in general results in abrupt movements when writing, affecting fluency.

○ A lack of confidence in spelling can restrict output.

○ A poor pencil grasp affects fluency.

○ Uncoordinated wrist movements result in stiffness and cramps. The principal movement in handwriting involves the flexion or extension synergy of the wrist and fingers to create a vertical elongation of letters. The sequences of letters themselves, and to some extent the horizontal component in their formation, are the result of these wrist actions.

○ A lack of kinaesthetic awareness produces slow writing through excess pressure and lack of limb awareness and sensation.

○ The child may become fatigued by the intensity of visual surveillance.

○ Difficulties in both central processing and kinaesthetic feedback may be evidenced by long intra-task pauses.

○ Reliance on visual feedback can restrict the fluency and spontaneity of handwriting.

○ Lack of somesthetic (interpretation of bodily sensation) feedback results in a tight pencil grip in order to provide some feedback from the joints as formations are executed.

○ As *compensation* for the lack of somesthetic feedback, further difficulties may arise – for example there is an over-reliance on vision, and eyes are fixed on the pencil point, the head close to the work.

Given the barriers that these children have to overcome and the additional physical and mental demands they face, it is not surprising that, whatever the cause of their particular difficulty, children who are struggling with handwriting at this stage often become despondent and reluctant writers.

Approaches to improving handwriting

A variety of approaches have been adopted over the years to try to help older children with handwriting problems – with mixed success.

One approach is to focus on letter formation, orientation and motor coordination. However, this developmental approach is not suitable for older children whose habits and patterns, however ineffective, are long established and hard to change.

Recognising the difficulty of changing established habits, some teachers adopt a more task-centred approach, with repeated practice of handwriting components and basic sequences in order to drill the child into producing accepted letter forms. Understandable though this might be, the underlying causes of the handwriting difficulty are not being addressed and this often leaves the child frustrated, resentful, antagonistic and increasingly self-conscious about their written presentation.

There are approaches that do begin to address underlying causes. One that has been successful with younger children is the perceptuo-motor programme *Write from the Start* (Teodorescu and Addy, 1996), which works on the perceptual processes while refining motor coordination. However, it is not usually as effective with the older age group, probably because perceptual conceptualisation tends to occur between the ages of 4 and 8 years. This does not mean that perceptual ability cannot be refined beyond this stage, but errors in visual interpretation usually prove more difficult to adjust.

A purely mechanical approach that addresses the physical aspect, and in particular pencil control, is of some value in this situation. Research has suggested that pencil grip and mechanics are significant factors in the speed of handwriting (Kao, 1973; Dooijes, 1983). However, although attending to these aspects may go some way to help control, it will not improve rhythm and fluency.

It is clear, therefore, that for older children experiencing handwriting difficulties, a completely different system is required. There is evidence from research and classroom practice to suggest that a kinaesthetic approach is most likely to be effective.

A kinaesthetic approach

Kinaesthesia is the awareness of the position and movement of limbs and joints – without the aid of visual feedback. Accuracy in kinaesthetic perception helps us to regulate pressure exerted through our limbs and to control our patterns of movement. In handwriting, accurate kinaesthetic perception is required in order to:

  ○ apply appropriate pressure through the writing instrument;

○ develop sensitivity to the patterns and rhythms required for producing cursive writing;

○ provide a non-visual image of the motor patterns required to form and join letters at speed.

Addressing underlying problems by improving kinaesthetic perception is the basis of the Speed Up! programme. It focuses on:

○ developing the muscle sense and mental image required to write fluently and at speed;

○ reducing dependence on visual attention to letter forms, replacing this with mental images reinforced by motor patterns and rhythmic movements which incorporate letter shapes and their connections;

○ freeing up the hand and arm, which may have become physically stiff as a result of undue tension and stress during writing;

○ internalising the rhythms and patterns of movement required to write at speed;

○ reducing anxiety.

The Speed Up! sessions comprise a series of activities, games and exercises that stimulate the joint sensors (proprioceptors) and arouse the body's kinaesthetic sense. This in turn sharpens movement sensitivity, motor acuity and pressure control. It also reduces tension in the arm and hand. At the same time as developing sensitivity to joint and limb position, the child is encouraged to develop a mental image of the patterns, movements and forms required for writing. As the child physically (rather than visually) experiences the rhythms and patterns of movement, skills are translated into faster and more fluent handwriting.

Writing speed

One of the consequences of a lack of kinaesthetic awareness and poor pressure control is a reduction in writing speed. Attempts to increase pace often increase the child's stress and tension and affect legibility. Researchers generally agree that girls write more quickly than boys (Alston, 1995; Dutton, 1992). This has been linked to physical maturity, with girls achieving maximum speed earlier than boys (Mason, 1991).

It is often difficult to ascertain exactly how slow a child's writing is in relation to that of their peers. In analysis of handwriting speed, there is considerable variation in the way speed is defined and assessed, but calculating words per minute is the most common measure. It is important to take into account writing stamina: over a prolonged period of time, fatigue sets in and writing speed decreases. Stamina is clearly of particular relevance for examinations.

One study found that a typical secondary-school pupil writes approximately one sentence of about 18 words, a quarter of which are multisyllabic, per minute. This rate can be maintained for at least 30 minutes. A writing rate of fewer than 12 words per minute would be considered abnormally low and would warrant help or additional time in examinations (Dutton, 1992).

Another study done with secondary-age pupils in the UK looked at how speed varies according to purpose: words per minute when neatness is required, words per minute when speed is required and words per minute under exam conditions (Mason, 1991). A summary of the results is given below.

Number of words written per minute for different purposes

	Neat	Quick	Exam
Female	11	17	18
Male	10	15	14
All	10	16	17

From Mason, 1991

A similar study concluded that writing increases in speed as the child rises to meet the demands of the secondary-school curriculum (Allcock, 2001). The results below show how the number of words per minute increased from Year 7 to Year 11.

Number of words written per minute by children from Year 7 to Year 11

Year 7	13.8
Year 8	14.3
Year 9	15.6
Year 10	14.7
Year 11	16.1

From Allcock, 2001

These results provide some guidance as to what can be expected for different age groups and what goals it might be appropriate to set for a child on the Speed Up! programme.

3 The kinaesthetic approach

In order to develop effective motor coordination, we need to have an effective sensory system. That is, we need a system of detectors that is sensitive to external stimuli and sufficiently finely tuned to provide the detailed information needed in order to make minute adjustments to movement, grip and touch. For example, to hold a pencil correctly, we must be able to apply the appropriate amount of pressure through our fingertips in order to grip the instrument in such a way that it can be easily manipulated. To secure this grip, we need to be able to feel the width and texture of the pencil barrel in order to bend our fingers to the appropriate position. We then need to assess how much tension is required in our muscles to maintain that grip. The necessary physical movements and adjustments are made only after the brain has processed information relayed by our sensory receptors. Of course, when we hold a pencil to write, none of these thoughts actually passes through our conscious mind; the process happens subconsciously and in a tiny fraction of a second.

The importance of kinaesthetic input

Sensory receptors in the muscles, joints and skin provide the central nervous system with detailed information about the position and movement of the limbs and body. They help us to interpret physical contact, applied pressure, static position and movement. All these receptor cells require some mechanical change in order to be stimulated. When we move a limb, for example, the receptors send information to the brain about what is moving and how much. The combined information from the different receptors provides us with a very precise mental 'map' of our limb positions and movements. This enables us to move with refined coordination and to carry out tasks without needing to look at what our hands, arms and legs are doing.

The four main sensory devices that are relevant for addressing handwriting difficulties are:

○ the proprioceptors of the articular surfaces (joints) – to relay specific information about pressure through the limbs and joint movement;

○ the proprioceptors embedded in the muscles and tendons – to relay information about pressure and muscle response;

○ the touch receptors in the cutaneous and deep-tissue surfaces – to detect subtle changes in pressure through the skin;

○ the vestibular complex (located in the inner ear and containing receptors that signal any head and trunk movement) – this helps us to maintain a stable, upright position, vital for performing fine-motor tasks.

The proprioceptors play a vital role in helping the child produce the fine-motor coordination needed for writing. They translate movement in order for the wrist and hand to travel across the page.

The vestibular system is important because handwriting involves the head and trunk just as much as the arms and hands. The head is required to move in order to scan the page and sometimes to look up at a board or to the side at a book. As the head moves, the trunk also moves in order to maintain a balanced position. Information from the vestibular receptors helps in stabilising the body and adjusting the posture in order to align the trunk, neck and head securely so that the upper limbs are free to move.

Complex fine-motor skills such as handwriting require high-level processing and memory of kinaesthetic input.

An important point to note is that kinaesthetic ability is dependent upon early experiences but also refined over the years. Certain skills cannot be fully generalised from one body part to another and are not fully developed in the hands until approximately 12 years of age. Up to this point, we have an opportunity to enhance and develop kinaesthetic awareness in relation to handwriting.

Kinaesthetic awareness and handwriting

Kinaesthetic feedback has two important functions in relation to handwriting.

First, it provides continuous information about the exact location of the upper limbs, about precise pressure through the handwriting instrument, and about patterns of movement. Information about patterns of movement and pressure is stored in our memory, to be recalled when we perform another similar movement. As we develop complex patterns of movement, such as those needed to produce handwriting, we are dependent upon the stored information in order to perform the associated motor actions. With practice, these patterns of movement become automatic, and so our attention can be directed to the composition aspect of writing rather than the mechanics of production. Adjustments are continually being made to refine motor coordination, and the new, adjusted movement generates its own kinaesthetic feedback which is subsequently stored in the motor memory. If the information received through the proprioceptive, cutaneous and vestibular systems is impaired, coordination will be poor, pressure through the writing instrument will be erratic and the pencil will be held tightly.

Second, kinaesthetic feedback reduces dependency on other sensory modalities such as vision (the strongest sense), and this happens increasingly as the child matures. To make the movement, the writer draws on the stored information in the motor memory. Thus the movement is automatic and also faster than if it relied on the processing of visual feedback. You can demonstrate the power of motor memory simply by writing your name with your eyes closed. Most people are able to produce a signature very close to their normal one because the movements required have been rehearsed many times and become automatic.

Signature written with eyes open

Charlotte Brown

Signature written with eyes closed

Charlotte Brown

The effects of poor kinaesthetic awareness

There are many children who, for reasons that are unknown, suffer from a degree of kinaesthetic impairment. In this category are children with dyspraxia and other perceptuo-motor disorders. For some reason, information from the various proprioceptors is transmitted incorrectly or not at all. It seems that the proprioceptors are either not as receptive as they ought to be or over-responsive. As a consequence, the child does not have the degree of motor control that would be expected for their age. Their limbs appear uncoordinated, movements are clumsy and control is laboured. Also, their inability to adjust pressure means they tend to grip tightly, exert heavy pressure through the upper limbs and lack controlled, fluent movement.

These difficulties are reflected in the child's handwriting, which is typically slow, with heavy pressure exerted through the writing instrument and jerky control. It has been suggested that kinaesthetic impairment in children might lead to slower handwriting, either because the child has to exert excessive pressure on the writing instrument to gain kinaesthetic information or because they are using visual feedback, which is slower than kinaesthetic feedback.

Poor kinaesthetic awareness also influences the patterns or flow of movement. Rhythmic patterns of motor control can only be achieved if adequate sensory input (in the form of proprioception, vestibular stimulation and touch) is available. Decreased sensory responsiveness will reduce rhythmic sensitivity and suppress the refined control of subsequent motor patterns. As cursive handwriting is dependent upon fluid, fluent letter forms which join together in regular patterns, the effect of poor kinaesthesia is obvious; the writing produced is hesitant and erratic and the writer appears to struggle with the connecting strokes that link letters together.

There is strong evidence to suggest that a lack of kinaesthetic sensitivity accounts for many handwriting difficulties, especially in the older child (for example Levine *et al.*, 1981).

Developing kinaesthetic awareness

If kinaesthetic awareness plays such an important role in the skill of handwriting, and poor kinaesthetic awareness has been shown to have a detrimental effect on handwriting, what, if anything, can be done to improve kinaesthetic awareness and, through that, the skill of handwriting?

Kinaesthetic acuity may be developed or enhanced by:

- developing an acute sense of limb location and position in the absence of vision by stimulating the body's upper limb proprioceptors;
- developing a non-visual awareness of movement and rhythm using bilateral upper-limb activities;
- encouraging kinaesthetic recall of letter forms and patterns, for example by writing letters in the air;
- reproducing consistent pre-writing patterns with vision occluded;
- developing a sense of movement flow as the arm moves away from the body;
- freeing up a potentially stiff arm and hand, increasing stamina and stability in the shoulder girdle;
- encouraging the application of kinaesthetic information to aid handwriting.

These principles are the basis of the activities and exercises in the Speed Up! programme.

Is the approach effective?

The results of research into the effectiveness of kinaesthetic training have been positive. Laszlo and Bairstow (1984) found demonstrable improvements in handwriting using a kinaesthetic training approach, as did Harris and Livesey (1992). Parents and teachers in a study by Sims *et al.* (1996) believed that kinaesthetic training had a significant effect on their children's handwriting. Teasdale *et al.* (1993) and Verschueren *et al.* (1999) also support the benefits of enhancing proprioception to improve fluency of handwriting.

Using the Speed Up! programme

The Speed Up! programme is carefully structured so that initially the child does not undertake any tasks that resemble formal handwriting. Instead, time is spent on kinaesthetic activities and exercises to promote non-visual sensory awareness of writing rhythms and patterns. This helps to counteract the effects of any previous unhelpful experiences involving repetition of hand–eye coordination writing tasks that concentrate on the visual aspects, often to the exclusion of other senses.

Programme objectives

The programme is structured around eight weekly sessions, each lasting 45–60 minutes.

The programme overview on pages 22–23 shows the progression in objectives.

Equipment

For the Speed Up! activities you will need various materials and resources. A few pieces of specialised equipment are required, but they can all be made relatively cheaply and are used repeatedly. In the course of the programme, you will use:

- a double-sided blackboard (see note on page 24);
- wax crayons, both chubby and thin;
- graphite pencils (B or 2B);
- marker pens;
- felt-tip pens in assorted thicknesses;
- ballpoint pens;
- rollerball pens;
- gel pens;
- light-up pens (these have a small bulb at the top which lights up if pressure is applied through the pen; they are available from many stationers);
- paint;

Objective	Activities	Week introduced
Stimulate the child's proprioceptive, sensory and vestibular systems to increase kinaesthetic awareness, in particular in the upper limbs.	Warm-up exercises.	1
Introduce the patterns of movement required for fluent writing using kinaesthetic training techniques.	Making patterns on a double-sided blackboard to stimulate bilateral hand and arm movements, whilst strengthening the shoulder girdle.	1
Free the hand, wrist and forearm in order to reduce stiffness and tension in preparation for writing.	Painting. Moving to music.	2 3
Reduce the stress and tension produced by the requirement to write quickly.	Competitive games involving a range of non-writing tasks and a variety of media and patterns of movement.	2
Introduce an element of rhythm and patterning in whole-body movement, which will gradually be channelled to patterning movements at the wrist and hand.	Making patterns that require gross-motor arm movements, by drawing on the double-sided blackboard. Painting on large sheets of paper. Moving to music.	2 2 3
Encourage the development of a mental (rather than actual) image of patterns of movement and form.	Reproducing sequences of movement with eyes closed; skywriting letter forms.	3
Use kinaesthetic feedback to develop patterns of movement; different proprioceptors are stimulated according to the level of pressure and vibration received.	Making patterns using a variety of drawing media, e.g. chalk, charcoal, wax crayon, pencil and felt-tip pen.	4

Objective	Activities	Week introduced
Link the kinaesthetic patterns to letter forms, developing rhythmicity in patterns.	Reproducing patterns of increasing complexity and basic letter forms repeatedly with eyes closed.	4
Develop fluency in cursive writing patterns, demonstrating how to 'feel' or judge hand position and comfort, and to determine when a break in the pattern is required.	Reproducing patterns using a variety of media.	4
	Thinking about the wrist and writing position in order to know when to move along the page.	4
Introduce writing words in cursive form.	Fun activities and competitive word games.	5
Develop fluency in cursive writing.	Producing handwriting by copying, from dictation and by composing own work.	6
	Word games.	7
Increase the speed of cursive writing.	Practising writing at speed.	6
Address the practical requirements of classroom writing.	Copying from a text, taking a dictation, writing freely on a subject chosen by the child and on a subject chosen by the trainer.	7

Programme overview

○ charcoal;

○ chalk, both white and coloured;

○ blackboard eraser

○ paintbrushes in assorted sizes;

○ sheets of newspaper;

○ large sheets of cheap paper (A1 and A2);

○ large sheets of sugar paper;

○ sheets of A4 paper, both plain and lined;

○ carbon paper;

○ rolls of bandage;

○ a CD player and CDs;

○ a video camera and player (optional);

○ photocopies of worksheets as needed.

Bearing in mind that several activities involve drawing or painting with eyes closed, you may want to check that you have tables with washable surfaces. If not, you can use newspaper to cover them.

Several of the activities use a double-sided blackboard, which can stand vertically. This can be made with a piece of wood 1 metre square and 45 mm thick, sanded and painted with blackboard paint, which can be bought from most DIY stores. The stand can be made simply from two strips of wood attached to a flat base. The board should slot into the stand snugly, without much wobble.

Double-sided blackboard and stand

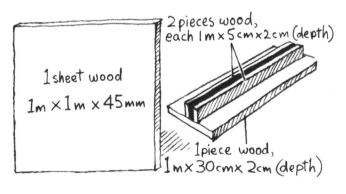

Position of the child at the double-sided blackboard

Alternatively, you could use one of the floor-standing double-sided blackboard easels available commercially. Again, the child needs to be positioned at the side of the board so that they can write on both sides simultaneously. They may need to sit down when writing on the lower part of the board.

Child standing at an easel-type blackboard. This can also be used by the child in a sitting position.

Group size

Programme sessions are best run with a small group of children; three is the ideal number. Children who are struggling with writing are more likely to become committed in a small group of others with similar difficulties. Frequently they are relieved to find they are not the only one struggling with this skill that others apparently find effortless. In this environment, they can be encouraged by reassurances that difficulty with handwriting is in no way a reflection on their intelligence. Often an element of friendly competition develops, which serves to boost motivation.

It is possible to run the programme on a one-to-one basis with an individual child, but some of the activities will need to be modified, sometimes with the trainer taking the part of another child. The child will need to be highly motivated to complete the activities and do the home practice.

Preparation

The programme begins with an initial assessment. As well as providing a baseline assessment, the checklist (see page 29) may be used to determine whether the programme is likely to benefit a particular child. The assessment should be carried out by the teacher or therapist, but the trainer leading the sessions could be a teaching assistant.

Also vital to the success of the programme is the preparation of the room and equipment. You should try to arrange for the sessions to take place in a separate room, away from other activity. There should be an area of free space available in the room in which the pupils can do the initial exercises. (Clearly, if the programme is being done with an individual child, less space is required.) Bear in mind that some sessions require the use of paint, so a sink area either within the room or somewhere nearby is helpful.

It is extremely important that each participating child has a suitable work station. This means a flat working surface of at least 1.5 metres width by 1 metre depth and a chair which will position their hips, knees and ankles at 90° angles with their feet placed firmly on the floor. The height of the work surface must be the distance from the floor to the base of the child's elbows when bent to 90°, when the child is seated on an appropriate chair. During the sessions the child will be either standing in front of or sitting at the work surface. If floor-standing blackboards are used, the child will sometimes need to move to stand and work there.

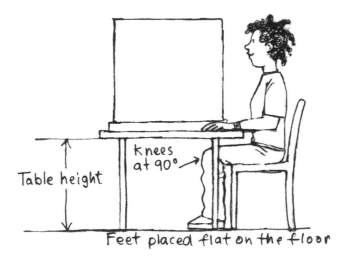

Correct seating position for writing

Assessment

The assessment of handwriting is often dependent upon non-standardised measures and the judgement of an individual professional. However, what constitutes good handwriting to one teacher may constitute poor writing to another. It is therefore important to have clear assessment criteria. By using an assessment tool, you can ensure that:

○ intervention provided is objectively evaluated;

○ the child is involved in setting personal goals based on objective information gained from the analysis of their handwriting (this is especially important when working with older children).

Before beginning the programme, you will need to do an assessment of each child's handwriting style and speed. This will serve as a baseline from which to work and will help to demonstrate improvement to the child at the end of the programme.

There are a number of standardised handwriting evaluation tools available which provide a detailed analysis of the varied components of handwriting. Further details of some of these are given on page 64. However, these are often time consuming to score and may provide more detail than is needed for the purposes of a programme such as this one. The assessment tool provided here is in the form of an observation checklist to use with the child's handwriting and classroom observation. It incorporates a measure of writing speed. If any of the statements on the observation checklist is ticked, then the Speed Up! programme is likely to be of benefit to the child.

To carry out the assessment, you need to obtain two samples of handwriting. First ask the child to write about a familiar topic for a period of 5 minutes. Make it clear that quantity and speed are not important. Use this first sample in conjunction with a copy of the checklist on page 29 to examine the style and fluency of the writing. The checklist also includes questions that will need to be answered through informal observation of the child while writing the sample.

Following this, or on a separate occasion, ask the child to write for a period of 5 minutes about a familiar topic which they choose themselves. This time they should aim to write as much as possible at fast speed. Use this second sample to calculate writing speed for the second part of the assessment on page 30.

Both samples can be attached to the child's checklist to form part of their record.

You may be interested to see how the Speed Up! programme can develop the child's kinaesthetic sense. This is particularly useful for children at secondary school who need to take notes rapidly from a board. To do this efficiently the writer needs to continue writing while looking at the board, relying on their kinaesthetic sense rather than their vision. The test of kinaesthetic acuity provided in the Appendix on pages 61–62 will enable you to assess what effect the programme has had on a child's kinaesthetic ability. Assessing the child before and after undertaking the programme will help you determine whether the programme has enhanced the child's kinaesthetic consciousness.

Setting goals

After completing the assessment, it is important to set objectives or goals. This can be done by choosing from the checklist those aspects of handwriting that are most in need of attention. If the assessment has revealed that the child's writing is slow, then you can also set a target for improving speed. See **Writing speed** on page 14 for guidance on expected speeds for different age groups.

Many older children are not really concerned about their handwriting, and feel irritated and frustrated by constant requests to write neatly. Asking a child to repeat work with better handwriting may simply increase their determination to offer the absolute minimum. It is vital, therefore, that the child is intrinsically motivated and wants to develop their handwriting. The fact that the programme does this through fun activities and not simply through yet more handwriting can help. It also helps if the child is personally involved in setting their own targets, even if it means settling for a set of objectives that are not exactly what you, as the teacher or therapist, would choose.

Ensure, however, that goals are realistic. For example, an 11-year-old might have a writing speed of 5 words a minute, indicated by the assessment. Although research indicates that a speed of around 13 to 14 words a minute could be expected at this age, it would be more realistic to set a target of 10 words a minute. It is better to set a target the child has a reasonable chance of achieving than to set one that is too high and risk almost certain failure.

The goals can be noted in the box on the assessment sheet. For some children, formalising your agreement on goals and commitment to the programme by means of a contract will help to increase motivation and the likelihood of their achieving the objectives. You could use the contract on page 31, or devise your own. You and the child might also agree on a reward for meeting their objectives.

Child's name _____ Age ____ years ____ months

Date of initial assessment _____

Date of subsequent assessment _____

Observation checklist

Consider each of the following statements using the first handwriting sample and classroom observation, as appropriate. Tick all that apply.

Characteristics	1st assessment ✓	2nd assessment ✓
Legibility is poor.		
Writing lacks a sense of rhythm.		
Writing appears laboured.		
Pressure applied through the writing instrument is either too light or too heavy.		
Writing is positioned above the line.		
Writing does not move horizontally across the page, but slopes either up or down.		
The first line of writing starts at the left and goes right across the page, but subsequent lines stray from the margin.		
When several sentences are written, lines merge.		
Writing is an inappropriate mixture of print and joined letters.		
Spaces between words are inadequate.		
Letter sizes are inconsistent.		
Some letters are incompletely formed.		
Some letters are joined inappropriately, e.g. the letter **o** is connected from its base.		
It is difficult to see clear ascending strokes on letters such as **k**, **d** and **t**.		
It is difficult to see clear descending strokes on letters such as **p** and **y**.		
Alignment of ascenders and descenders is erratic: some slant forwards, some backwards, and some are upright.		

Speed Up! Handwriting assessment

Writing speed

Count the number of words in the second handwriting sample, then divide the number of words by 5 to obtain the number of words per minute.

Number of words in writing sample _____

Number of words per minute _____

Goals

Speed Up! Contract

Name _____

Age _____

School _____

I agree to complete the Speed Up! handwriting programme.

I will do my Speed Up! practice

at least _____ times a week.

I aim to increase my handwriting speed

from _____ words a minute

to _____ words a minute.

I also aim to improve

_____.

Signed _____

Supported by _____

Date _____

Case study

Gemma is a 9-year-old girl who was struggling with handwriting. A sample of her writing was assessed using the checklist and a list of goals was written in collaboration with Gemma.

Maddy Roberts lived whith her Mother in a small town beside the lee the Sea Their house looked odenery eghas but a sign haning above the font door told everone that it wos feny ahotel the belmot Praivte

Speed Up! Handwriting assessment

29

Child's name _____Gemma_____   Age _9_ years _0_ months

Date of initial assessment _____

Date of subsequent assessment _____

Observation checklist

Consider each of the following statements using the first handwriting sample and classroom observation, as appropriate. Tick all that apply.

Characteristics	1st assessment ✓	2nd assessment ✓
Legibility is poor.		
Writing lacks a sense of rhythm.	✓ mixture of joined writing and print	
Writing appears laboured.		
Pressure applied through the writing instrument is either too light or too heavy.		
Writing is positioned above the line.		
Writing does not move horizontally across the page, but slopes either up or down.	✓ veers downwards	
The first line of writing starts at the left and goes right across the page, but subsequent lines stray from the margin.	✓	
When several sentences are written, lines merge.	✓ evident in other samples	
Writing is an inappropriate mixture of print and joined letters.		
Spaces between words are inadequate.	✓ occasionally	
Letter sizes are inconsistent.	✓	
Some letters are incompletely formed.		
Some letters are joined inappropriately, e.g. the letter o is connected from its base.	✓ s	
It is difficult to see clear ascending strokes on letters such as **k**, **d** and **t**.		
It is difficult to see clear descending strokes on letters such as **p** and **y**.	✓ f and p	
Alignment of ascenders and descenders is erratic: some slant forwards, some backwards, and some are upright.	✓	

© Speed Up! LDA

Speed Up! Handwriting assessment

30

Writing speed

Count the number of words in the second handwriting sample, then divide the number of words by 5 to obtain the number of words per minute.

Number of words in writing sample _____40_____

Number of words per minute _____8_____

Goals

1. To develop fluency and rhythm in order to encourage consistent sizing of letters

2. To encourage clear demarcation between the size of letters, particularly descending letters

3. To start each line at the right side of the page and transfer across in a horizontal direction

4. To increase speed of output to 10 words per minute

© Speed Up! LDA   Permission to Photocopy

Leading the sessions

Ideally the sessions should take place weekly at a regular time and place. The training is intensive and consistency helps the children to understand the commitment required and to get into a practice routine.

Whether the sessions are led by you, as teacher or therapist, or by a teaching assistant, it is important for the trainer to read through the instructions for each session in advance so that they are familiar with the activities and have the necessary resources assembled. A list of equipment needed is given at the beginning of each session. The instructions may be photocopied as required for use by the trainer.

Suggested timings are given for each of the activities, but these are all approximate as the time taken will vary according to the age, ability and motivation of the group or individual child.

Each session lasts approximately 1 hour. If shorter sessions are preferred, each one may be split and delivered as two sessions. Each one would need to begin with the warm-up exercises and homework review, and would last approximately 40 minutes.

In order to gain any benefit from the programme, it is vital that children do the homework, including the warm-up exercises. They should do this at least three times a week and ideally they should do a little each day. If possible, children should also be given the opportunity to use the double-sided blackboard as part of their practice. In a primary school, a board may be left in the classroom or other area and the children given a few minutes to practise a couple of times each day. In a secondary school, it may be necessary to provide a board for each child to take and use at home.

An important aspect of this programme is improving pupils' motivation and confidence. Many children will have experienced handwriting difficulties for a number of years and now view writing with apprehension and concern. Some have the motivation and determination to do better – if only they could be shown how. Others have become switched off and another writing programme is the last thing they want to do. When this is the case, the trainer will need to be able to see through the coping strategies and reinstate the child's confidence and commitment with sensitivity. The success of the programme rests, therefore, not only on following the regime of exercises and activities, but also on the enthusiasm and encouragement of the trainer.

Ending the programme and evaluation

At the end of the programme, it can be expected that all pupils who have fully participated in the sessions will have made some progress. After the last weekly session has been completed, obtain fresh samples of handwriting in exactly the same way as for the initial assessment, and carry out a second assessment. Together with the child, review the results in relation to the first assessment and the contract, if one was made. Decide whether the goals have been achieved.

If the goals have been achieved, discuss with the child the strategies they can use to maintain their improvement (see **After the programme**, on page 36).

If goals have not been achieved there are several possible reasons. Use the list below to identify the most likely reason and agree an appropriate course of action.

○ The goals agreed may have been unrealistic. Failure to achieve objectives can leave a child feeling frustrated and disappointed. If this happens it is worth investigating which aspect of handwriting the child is continuing to struggle with, for example speed, fluency or rhythm. If the expected speed has not been achieved, repeat the sessions from Week 5 onwards, setting more specific, smaller and achievable targets. If fluency is still lacking, consider an alternative handwriting approach such as Write Dance by Ragnhild Oussoren Voors. If rhythm of writing remains poor, consider Callirobics™ by Liora Laufer (see page 64 for details).

○ The programme may not have been followed closely. The programme is progressive in nature and it is therefore important that all the tasks are done in the correct order, including the physical activities that commence each session. These are crucial in stimulating the upper limb proprioceptors prior to commencing graphic training. It may be tempting to introduce additional tasks that seem more directly related to handwriting too early, but the success of the approach depends on the child developing kinaesthetic awareness through the foundational exercises without being constrained by the demands of more formal writing tasks.

The child may not have done the practice at home. If this is so, try to ascertain the reasons. If practising at home is difficult, for whatever reason, consider whether it is possible to provide a time and place for practice within school. Ideally this would be every day, but three times a week may be more realistic. Once a school practice time has been agreed, the child repeats the whole programme.

○ The child may have a problem known as general hypotonia. In this condition (described by Summers, 2001) it is lax, floppy muscles – rather than the lack of kinaesthetic ability – that affect the child's motor control. In this situation, the Speed Up! programme will enhance the stamina and fluency of the handwriting, but increase in speed may not be as marked as in other children. Where general hypotonia is a problem, consider introducing the child to word-processing and keyboard skills as well.

○ Children's progress may be limited by physical changes as they approach puberty. Both sexes, but boys in particular, go through a period of rapid growth during which they may become clumsy and uncoordinated. Hormonal changes can influence motivation and self-esteem, perhaps more so in girls.

○ The child may have been insufficiently motivated and simply not want to improve their handwriting. It is therefore important to identify exactly what will motivate them. Do they prefer to word-process written information? If so, should the provision of a computer be considered? Is the child struggling with the group approach in the programme? If so, can it be implemented on a one-to-one basis? You should also consider whether the child has been fully involved in goal setting; motivation is likely to be lowered if they have had standards imposed upon them.

○ Some children, especially those reaching puberty, have so much physical and emotional change to contend with, that improving handwriting is the last thing on their agenda. They may need to be reminded of the importance of handwriting for the completion of assessed work. Some may also need time to consider the options before returning to the programme.

○ A few children may have such difficulty interpreting sensory information that they require a more intense approach known as 'sensory integration' (Ayres, 1979). These children have extremely poor pressure adjustment through the writing instrument, caused by inadequate proprioception. In addition they may appear physically unstable during non-visual activities; this demonstrates dysfunctional vestibular regulation. These children may be over-reliant on vision and really struggle to coordinate movements when vision is occluded. Sensory integration is a specialist approach and therefore additional advice should be sought from either the paediatric occupational therapist or the physiotherapist at the local Child Development Centre.

After the programme

After completing the programme, children should be encouraged to put techniques learned into practice. In a primary school setting, it may be possible to incorporate the warm-up exercises as a whole-class routine, either at the beginning of the day or before a writing activity. Otherwise, children can perform the forearm triggers (Activity 1) sitting in their seats before starting any written work. At secondary level, children can be encouraged to do the seated forearm triggers before writing tasks in lessons and also to do the full set of exercises before doing written homework at home. If subject teachers are informed about the programme, they can remind children to do the warm-ups at appropriate moments.

As the child progresses and develops fluency and speed, these exercises can be gradually reduced, although it can be helpful to continue with the forearm triggers. If a child's newly developed fluency subsequently deteriorates, perhaps during periods of extra pressure of work or after a long break such as the summer holidays, returning to exercises on the double-sided board is a good way of regaining the necessary movements and rhythm. Patterning to music using a variety of writing materials is also effective. These may need to be adopted for a short period only, for example two weeks following a break or each evening during a period of examinations.

Games included in the programme can be revisited either as a class activity or at home with the family. These can reinforce the idea that writing, despite being a complex skill, can be fun.

These exercises should be undertaken at the start of each session and will take about 10 minutes in total. They should also be practised as part of homework during the course of the programme. Ideally children should continue to use them prior to any handwriting activity, both at school and at home; clearly it will not always be possible to carry out all the activities in every situation, but children should be encouraged to use the forearm triggers in Activity 1.

The warm-up exercises are key to the success of the programme, so it is vital that children learn to do them correctly. By continuing with the exercises after completing the programme, the child will maintain the benefits of enhanced joint awareness.

Activity 1 consists of two 'sensory triggers' that will heighten the sensitivity of the proprioceptors of the upper limbs whilst encouraging shoulder girdle stability. They have the effect of improving pressure adjustment through the upper limbs for about 40 minutes, after which the sensitivity appears to subside. After doing the exercises, the child would therefore be expected to demonstrate improved awareness of pressure application through the writing instrument, an essential aspect of maintaining fluency and speed.

Activity 1 Forearm triggers

○ The child pushes their body up from the seat, as shown. Encourage the child to do as many of these as they can each week. By the end of the programme, most children should be able to manage 10 or more.

Independent triggers

○ Many children may be able to manage only four or five independent triggers at first, in which case you should stimulate the receptors further by performing assisted triggers as follows.

○ Hold the child's arm in an extended (straight) position, held out at a slight angle to the body, the elbow straight.

○ Hold the hand and wrist while supporting the elbow, as shown in the diagram. Push the arm towards the body in a gentle jerking movement.

○ Do this 10 times for each arm, taking care not to push too hard.

Triggers with partner assisting

Activity 2 Shoulder girdle spirals

○ The child holds both arms out horizontally to the side and begins to circle them, initially making small circles but gradually getting larger until the circles are as large as possible. This should take about five rotations.

○ When the circles have reached full size, change the direction and gradually reduce the circles, again taking about 5 rotations, to get back to the smallest size.

○ Aim to repeat 10 times but take care not to over-stress the limbs. At the start of the programme, the child may only manage as few as 4 spiral sequences before tiring. Encourage them to practise and to build up the number, as this will improve their stamina in writing.

Shoulder spirals

Activity 3 Half push-ups

○ The child lies face down on the floor and pushes the body up with their arms in the same way as a normal press-up, but keeping the tummy on the floor. Some children may be able to lift the tummy away from the floor and they can be encouraged to do this, if and when they are able. (Some children may not be able to achieve this.)

○ Repeat 10 times.

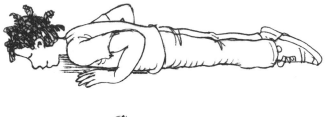

Half push-ups

Activity 4 Wall press-ups

○ Ask the child to face a wall and stand about $1\frac{1}{2}$ arms' lengths away from it.

○ Ask them to stretch out their arms, keeping them at shoulder level, and place their hands flat on the wall. They should then try to bring their face to the wall without moving their feet.

○ Keeping the body straight, they straighten the arms, pushing themselves away from the wall.

○ Repeat 10 times.

Wall press-ups

Activity 5 Creeping thumbs

- ○ For this you need a bandage, about 75 cm long. With the child seated at a table, place the unrolled bandage in front of them, stretching it out horizontally as shown in the diagram.

- ○ Ask the child to put their writing hand at one end of the bandage, placing it on the right-hand end if they are right-handed and on the left-hand end if they are left-handed. The hand should be positioned with the fingers resting on the bandage and the palm on the table, as shown in the diagram. Then ask them to see if they can gather up the bandage, tucking it under their hand, using the thumb of that hand only and keeping the wrist still.

- ○ Ask them to do this 5 times, seeing if they can increase their speed each time.

- ○ To make this more interesting for younger children, you could draw features on the bandage such as those shown below.

Creeping thumbs

Activity 6 Creepy crawlies

- ○ With the child seated at a table, place an unrolled bandage in front of them, this time stretching it out vertically as shown in the diagram.

- ○ Ask the child to place their hand on the end of the bandage nearest them to anchor it. The child tries to gather the bandage up, keeping the wrist still and using the fingers of that hand only. The fingers move together to pull the bandage in.

- ○ Get them to do this 5 times, seeing if they can increase their speed each time.

- ○ As in Activity 5, features may be drawn on the bandage for younger children.

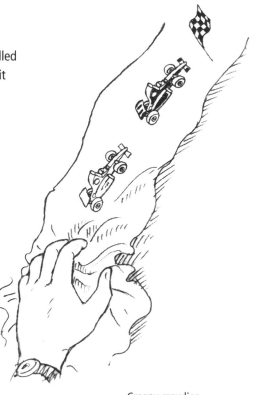

Creepy crawlies

Equipment

Double-sided blackboards, chalks, blackboard erasers, large sheets of sugar paper, marker pens, tape

1 Warm-up exercises

  ○ Begin the session by teaching the children the warm-up exercises.   (20 minutes)

2 Double-sided blackboard

  ○ Seat the children at tables. (See the instructions on page 26 for correct positioning.) Place a double-sided blackboard in front of each child so that they cannot see the surfaces of the board and give each child two pieces of chalk so they can hold one in each hand.

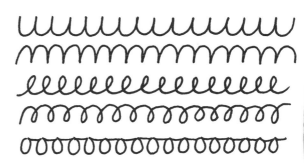

Patterns for double-sided blackboard

  ○ Tell the children that they are going to make the same pattern simultaneously on each side of the board. Explain that they will not be able to see the patterns they are creating but that their body is sending messages to their brain about the movements their arms are making – and that these messages are called kinaesthetic feedback. Explain that this exercise, like many of the others they will be doing, will improve their kinaesthetic feedback, which will, in turn, help their handwriting.

  ○ Introduce the first pattern in the set above. First demonstrate the pattern on a board, then guide each child's hands through the movement on the double-sided blackboard, starting at the near side of the board and travelling away from the body. Then ask the children to fill both sides of the board with rows of the pattern.

  ○ Repeat the process for each of the other four patterns.

  ○ Children should aim for even, horizontal patterns of consistent size. They may find this difficult and tiring at first and patterns will probably slope downwards. Encourage them to persevere so they can build up the stamina that will also help their handwriting.

○ Each time they fill a board with a pattern, ask the children to look at it and say what it reminds them of. They can then add some drawing to the pattern to turn it into a picture. For example, if they think the first pattern looks like waves on the sea, they could add boats and sharks' fins.

○ When they have done all the patterns, ask the children to stand up and repeat the activity in a standing position, keeping the board in the same place.

(15–20 minutes)

3 Double-sided blackboard and paper

○ Cover the boards on each side with a large sheet of sugar paper, securing it with tape. Ask the children to repeat all the patterns in the same way as before, using one sheet for each pattern and again using chalk. Explore with the child whether the surfaces made any difference to their movements.

○ Cover the boards with fresh sheets of sugar paper and ask the children to repeat all the patterns, again using one sheet for each pattern but this time using marker pens.

○ Ask the children whether the medium made any difference to their movements. The rough surface of the sugar paper increases the friction, slowing down the movement and requiring the child to exert more effort through the upper limbs. The increase in pressure and vibration helps to trigger the receptors in the arm muscles; this helps them to feel the movement more, which in turn helps to develop fluent handwriting. If children have not noticed that more effort is needed, check whether they are applying enough pressure and repeat the activity if necessary.

○ For both the chalk and marker patterns, children can add features to their patterns if they wish.

(15–20 minutes)

Homework

Remind children that they have agreed to practise at least three times during the week and every day if possible. Or, if contracts have been used, remind the children about the amount of practice they each agreed to do.

Explain that they should always remember to do the warm-up exercises before starting the homework tasks.

Tell them that this week, their task is to practise making the patterns on the double-sided blackboard.

Equipment

Double-sided blackboards, chalks, blackboard erasers, large sheets of cheap paper (A2) or large sheets of newspaper, paint, thick paintbrushes, water pots, wax crayons (chubby variety), thick marker pens

1   Warm-up exercises
    ○   Begin the session by doing the warm-up exercises. (10 minutes)

2   Homework review
    ○   Ask the children how they got on with practising at home. Ask them to demonstrate how they have progressed with using the double-sided blackboard by making all five patterns. Look together at the size, consistency and alignment of the patterns and ask them to see which are the clearest, most consistent rows of pattern. Have these been made by their dominant hand? (5 minutes)

3   Paint a sheet of paper
    ○   This activity helps to free up the wrist and hands. Place a large sheet of paper on each table and ask the children to cover their sheets of paper with paint, using a thick paintbrush. Encourage them to cover the paper completely, brushing in any direction they choose and taking as much time as they want.
    ○   Now give out fresh sheets of paper and ask them to repeat the activity, this time covering the sheet as quickly as possible.
    ○   Repeat the activity once more, this time making it a competition. The children race against each other to cover the paper. (You should participate if this programme is not undertaken in a group.) (10–15 minutes)

4   Paint a shape
    ○   On each table, place a large sheet of paper on which you have drawn a simple shape, such as the one shown below. Ask the children to paint the shape as fast as possible, filling it completely and keeping within the lines.

○ Give each child a fresh sheet of paper with a more complex shape, such as the one shown below. Again ask the child to paint it as fast as possible, keeping within the lines.

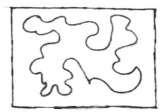

○ Repeat the activity with complex shapes, this time making it a competition. Each child draws a shape which is then given to another child to paint. They race against each other to fill the shape. (You should participate if this programme is not undertaken in a group.)   (10–15 minutes)

5   Crayon a shape

○ Repeat the whole of Activity 4, filling the shapes with crayons instead of paint.

(10–15 minutes)

6   Continuous scribble

○ Place a large sheet of paper on each table. Ask the children to close their eyes and try to fill the page with slow circular scribbles, using a wax crayon. They should try not to stop or lift their pen, but to keep their hand moving steadily and continuously in a spiral pattern. You may need to tell the child when to stop.

○ Repeat the activity, this time using marker pens instead of crayons.   (10 minutes)

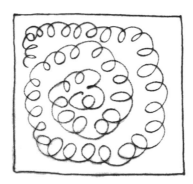

Homework

Ask the children to do the following activities during the week:

○ Continue to practise patterns using the double-sided blackboard.

○ Practise circular scribbles on a large sheet of paper, as in Activity 6.

○ On a large sheet of paper, draw a picture using circular movements.

Remind the children to continue with the warm-up exercises before each practice.

Ask them to bring their work to the next session. Ask them also to bring some CDs of their favourite music.

Equipment

Video camera (optional), CD player and CDs, large sheets of cheap paper, wax crayons (chubby variety)

1 Warm-up exercises

- Begin the session by doing the warm-up exercises. (10 minutes)

2 Homework review

- Review homework with the children, asking how they got on with the activities. (4–5 minutes)

3 Place your arms without looking

- Put the children into pairs. (You will need to participate as one of a pair if there is only one child or an odd number.) The first child in each pair stands up straight with their eyes closed and their arms at their sides. The other child moves their arms into a position, which is held for a count of three before returning them to the sides of the body. Keeping their eyes closed, the first child repeats the action without guidance.

- Repeat this several times, taking the arms to a different position each time. Then the pair swap roles. (5 minutes)

4 Move your arms without looking

- Children stay in the same pairs. The first child in each pair stands up straight with their eyes closed and their arms at their sides. Their partner takes the arms through a short sequence of three or four movements, then returns them to the sides. Keeping their eyes closed, the first child repeats the sequence of movement without guidance.

- Repeat this several times, changing the movement sequence each time. Then the pair swap roles. This can be videoed to demonstrate the accuracy of repositioning. (10 minutes)

5 Skywriting
- Ask each child in turn to choose a letter from the alphabet, draw it in the air with their finger and then ask the others to guess the letter. Extend this to drawing words in the air. (This activity could also be done in pairs.) (5 minutes)

6 Move to the music
- Before the session, select some pieces of music with a distinctive beat. This can be any piece with a strong beat that is not too fast; many tracks by Vangelis work well, as does 'We All Stand Together' by Paul McCartney! You can also use some tracks from the CDs the children have brought in. It certainly helps to use something that suits their own musical tastes; just check that any track you use has a strong beat at a suitable speed.
- Show the children how to tap the beat of the music quite simply with an up and down movement. Ask them to continue the movement with their eyes closed. Repeat the activity using pieces of music with a different beat.
- Play some more pieces of music with a strong beat. This time ask the children to close their eyes and to beat the rhythm of the music onto the table. Again repeat the activity, using several different pieces of music. (10 minutes)

7 Draw to the music
- Place a large sheet of paper and some wax crayons on each table. Play some more music with a strong beat. Choose one of the five patterns introduced in session 1 and show children how to draw it to the music, moving their crayon according to the beat. Encourage them to feel the beat in their hands and to break the pattern, raising and lowering the crayon when they feel it is appropriate, for example between lines in a song or between musical phrases.
- Choose a piece of music which a child has brought in and ask them to make some more patterns to the music. Ask the children to choose one of the patterns from session 1, thinking about which one best suits. Repeat the activity with different types of music. (15 minutes)

Homework

Ask the children to do the following activities during the week:
- Continue to practise patterns using the double-sided blackboard.
- Choose a piece of music you like. With your eyes closed, move your arms according to the beat. You could make up a hand jive.
- Choose a piece of music and practise making patterns to the beat.
- Choose a piece of music which has a strong beat, to bring to the next session.

Remind children to bring the work they have done at home to the next session.

Equipment

CD player and CDs, large sheets of cheap paper, wax crayons (chubby variety), a copy of Worksheet A for each child, a selection of drawing instruments (e.g. charcoal, chalk, felt-tip pen, pencil), plain A4 paper, very large sheets of paper (approximately A1), graphite pencils (B or 2B), paint and thick paintbrushes

1 Warm-up exercises
- ○ Begin the session by doing the warm-up exercises. (10 minutes)

2 Homework review
- ○ Review homework with the children, discussing how they got on with patterning to music and looking at samples. (4–5 minutes)

3 Move to the music
- ○ Choose a piece of music brought in by a child. Ask the children to listen with their eyes closed and beat their hands on the table in time to the music.
(5 minutes)

4 Draw to the music
- ○ Give each child a copy of Worksheet A. Play a piece of music and discuss which of the five patterns in the top box would best fit the music. Ask the children, with their eyes closed, to draw that pattern to the music using wax crayons on large sheets of paper. Encourage the children to sense when it is appropriate to lift their wrist from the page in order to move across the paper.
(10 minutes)

- ○ Repeat the activity, this time asking the children to use different drawing instruments (e.g. charcoal, chalk, felt-tip pen, pencil). Discuss the different movement and pressure required for each. They are likely to say that writing with a felt-tip pen is easier than with chalk or charcoal. This is because there is less friction and so it takes less effort. This can lead into a discussion about preferred writing instruments and which the children find most comfortable in terms of friction and fluency. Change the music to add variety. (10 minutes)

5 Change the pressure
- ○ Give each child a pencil and a piece of paper (A4 size). Ask them, with their eyes open, to draw patterns from Activity 4 across the page, making rows with alternate light and heavy pressure. Discuss with them how pressure changes the fluency of the movement. (5 minutes)

6 Group pattern

○ End with a collaborative game in which the group make a picture together. Cover a table or group of tables with a very large sheet of a paper and ask the children to sit round it. Explain that you will play some music and that they must paint patterns to the beat of the music, choosing from the patterns used in Activity 4. After a short while, stop the music and ask them to move according to your instructions (for example move one place to the right or two places to the left). Encourage them to paint in the spaces and not to overlap other people's patterns. Play a number of pieces of music until the children have moved places about seven or eight times and the paper is filled. The end result should be a collaborative picture made up of rhythmic patterns. Look together at the way the different patterns express the music. (15 minutes)

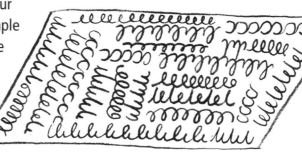

7 New patterns

○ Ask the children to look at the patterns in the middle box of Worksheet A and to try them out with crayons on sheets of plain paper. Explain that they will be using these new patterns in this week's homework.

ccccccccccccccc

olololololololololololo

ssssssssssssssss

ggggggggggggggg

Homework

Ask the children to do the following activities during the week:

○ Continue to practise patterns using the double-sided blackboard.

○ With eyes closed, use crayons to fill a sheet with the patterns in the middle box on Worksheet A. Draw in some features to make the patterns into a picture – use your imagination!

Ensure children have copies of Worksheet A to take home and remind children to bring the work they have done at home to the next session.

cccccccccccccc

Worksheet A

Session 5

Equipment

Graphite pencils (B or 2B), plain A4 paper, one copy of Worksheet A and two copies of Worksheet B for each child, CD player and CDs, large sheets of paper (A2), felt-tip pens, stopwatch or timer, light-up pens (for homework)

1   Warm-up exercises

○   Begin the session by doing the warm-up exercises.   (10 minutes)

2   Homework review

○   Review homework with the children, looking at the patterns they have produced.

(4–5 minutes)

3   Draw to the music

○   Give each child a copy of Worksheet A and a sheet of A4 paper. Ask them to make patterns to music, using a pencil and with their eyes closed. They should use patterns from the top box on Worksheet A, choosing ones to suit the music.

○   The children repeat the activity with their eyes open. Discuss whether it feels any different from doing it with eyes closed. They may notice that when their eyes are open, they are more aware of what the pattern looks like and of the pressure being applied, which may slow them down. Encourage them to 'feel' the flow of the pattern – as they do when they have their eyes closed – rather than concentrating on the appearance of the shape.   (10 minutes)

4   Writing patterns

○   Give each child a copy of Worksheet B. Ask them to use a pencil to continue each pattern, keeping on the guide lines and taking as much time as they want.

○   Give each child a second copy of Worksheet B. This time, ask them to complete the patterns as fast as possible, either against the clock or competing with a partner.

○   Ask the children to look at the patterns in the bottom box on Worksheet A. Ask them to make each one with a pencil on a sheet of A4 paper, first with eyes closed and then with eyes open.   (20–30 minutes)

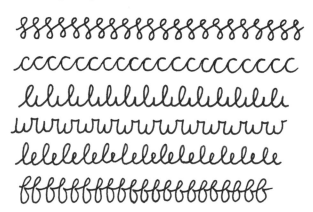

Up to now, the children have been practising patterns of joined letter forms; in the next two activities, they will start to use writing for the first time in the programme. You should encourage the children to use cursive writing for all the writing activities, joining all letters appropriately.

5 Calligrams

○ Demonstrate how to make a calligram or word picture; you could use either of the examples below. Then ask the children to create some of their own, first writing the words as smoothly as possible with a felt-tip pen on a large sheet of paper (approximately A3), then adding the features.   (10 minutes)

6 Just a minute

○ Give out sheets of plain A4 paper. Explain to the children that they are going to have 1 minute to write as many words as they can on a particular subject. Show them the example below. Ask a child to think of the first subject and as soon as they have announced it, everyone begins writing. All words must be written in a joined script (looped or non-looped style). If you wish, you can score by awarding one point for each relevant word in legible, cursive script.

Valentine's Day

hearts	soppy	hearts	soppy
love	red	love	red
postman	flowers	postman	flowers
roses	perfume	roses	perfume
February	cards	February	cards

Looped style   Non-looped style

○ Repeat the game, with other members of the group taking turns to suggest a subject.   (5 minutes)

Homework

Give each child a light-up pen to take home and ask them to do the following activities during the week:

○ Continue to practise patterns using the double-sided blackboard.

○ Play Just a minute with a family member or friend.

○ Using the light-up pen, write one or two sentences about how you feel about handwriting. When used with normal writing pressure, the light goes on and off with the slight variation in pressure. If the light is either on all the time or off all the time, then the pressure is either too heavy or too light. Explain this to the children and ask them to watch what happens when they do the writing for homework.

Remind children to bring the work they have done at home to the next session.

Worksheet B

uuuu

llll

cccc

ununun

rrrrr

elelele

ssss

oooo

ssss

uuuu

vvvv

aaaa

Equipment

Two copies of Worksheet C for each child, a choice of writing instruments including graphite pencils, felt-tip pens, ballpoint pens, rollerball pens and gel pens, plain A4 paper, lined A4 paper, a book for dictation

1 **Warm-up exercises**

○ Begin the session by doing the warm-up exercises. (10 minutes)

2 **Homework review**

○ Look at the sentences written for homework and discuss how monitoring the pressure with the light-up pens influenced their handwriting. If they are writing with too little or too much pressure, encourage them to keep practising with the light-up pen to correct it. (4–5 minutes)

3 **Writing patterns**

○ Give each child a copy of Worksheet C. Ask them to continue each pattern, keeping on the guide lines and taking as much time as they want. Children can make their own choice of writing instrument.

○ Give each child a second copy of Worksheet C. This time, ask them to complete the patterns as fast as possible, either against the clock or competing with a partner. (10–15 minutes)

4 **Writing without looking**

○ Ask the children to hold their pencils near the tip (right next to the paper) and write their name with their eyes closed. Get them to repeat this, holding the pencil approximately 2 cm away from the tip. Discuss how the change in grip influenced control. They may notice that if the writing instrument is held too near to the tip, the pressure increases, the letters tend to get smaller and it is difficult to see the writing being produced. In this position, writing slows down and becomes laboured. However, if the instrument is held too far away from the tip, the pressure decreases, more effort is required from the shoulders and it is harder to exercise control. In this position, control and legibility deteriorate.

○ Give each child a sheet of A4 paper and a pencil. Ask them to close their eyes and write down a short passage from a book, which you will dictate to them slowly. (Use something that they will enjoy.) When they have finished, discuss how the writing looks and how it felt.

○ Repeat the activity with a different passage from the book, this time with the children keeping their eyes open. Afterwards, discuss with the children how it felt. Did their tension increase? Did that affect pressure through the pencil?

(20 minutes)

Session 6

5 Write for a minute

○ Ask the children to think of a poem or the words of a song that they know by heart. Give them some lined A4 paper and ask them to write from memory as much as they can in 1 minute. Count how many words were written.

○ Ask the children to write as much as they can in a minute on a topic of their own choice. Again, count the number of words written.

○ Check these scores against the initial assessments to see how speed is developing. Look also at each child's goals to see if they are on track for achieving their objectives.

(10 minutes)

Homework

○ Continue to practise patterns using the double-sided blackboard.

○ Ask a family member to recite a poem or a tongue twister. Try to write it down as quickly and fluently as possible.

Remind children to bring the work they have done at home to the next session.

Worksheet C

aaaa

bbbb

eeee

ffff

hhhh

jjjj

kkkk

rrrr

ssss

cccc

yyyy

gggg

Session 7

Equipment

A copy of Worksheet D for each child, three copies of Worksheet E for each child, wax crayons, a choice of writing instruments including graphite pencils, felt-tip pens, ballpoint pens, rollerball pens and gel pens, plain A4 paper, lined A4 paper, books for copying from

1 Warm-up exercises

○ Begin the session by doing the warm-up exercises.   (10 minutes)

2 Homework review

○ Look at the poems and tongue twisters written out for homework.

(4–5 minutes)

3 Speed colouring

○ Give each child a copy of Worksheet D and ask them to colour the picture as quickly as possible, using different colours for different sections and keeping within the lines.   (10–15 minutes)

4 Writing with and without looking

○ Give the children some plain A4 paper and a selection of writing instruments to choose from. Ask the children to close their eyes, then write in cursive script a sentence you dictate. Look at the result together and discuss progress.

○ Give the children some lined A4 paper and ask them to copy a paragraph from a book, writing as fluently and neatly as possible. Discuss whether they encountered any difficulties in this activity. If they found it hard to keep their place while copying, suggest they put a piece of card under the sentence being copied, blocking out the rest of the paragraph. Talk about where the book is positioned in relation to the writing and where it is most comfortable. It may help to have the book propped up slightly.

○ Ask the children to compose a paragraph describing an event that took place whilst on holiday. They should write this in a cursive script, with their eyes closed. Discuss whether it was easier to write when copying or when composing.   (20 minutes)

5 Word consequences

○ Each group member has a sheet of plain A4 paper and a pencil. Ask them to write down (in cursive sript) either a boy's name or the name of a famous man at the top of the paper. They then fold the paper over to prevent anyone seeing and pass it to the person on their right. Then ask everyone to write the name of a girl or famous woman. Continue in this way, working down the list of categories below. When you have reached the final category, the papers are handed on for the last time. Players then unfold the papers and take turns to read out the stories. Alternatively, collect them in and read them out yourself. Clearly in order for this to work, all contributions must be legible!

- (Boy's name)
- met (girl's name)
- whilst (a hobby or something you enjoy)
- (at/in) a favourite place.
- He said to her, (a question).
- She said to him, (a reply).
- They both became (what you'd like to be in the future)
- and (something you'd like to do in the future).   (10 minutes)

6 Initial letter game

- This gives children practice in writing specific letters while undertaking a challenge. Give out Worksheet E, then give the children an initial letter. Everyone must write down in cursive script a word beginning with that letter for each category. Children can write with the instrument of their choice. The competition can be timed or untimed. Children swap sheets for marking and points are awarded as follows:
  1 point for each appropriate word
  2 points for an appropriate word not chosen by anyone else.   (10 minutes)

Homework

Give each child two copies of Worksheet E to do at home with a family member. Explain that they should mark them at home and bring them to the next session.

Remind them to continue to make patterns using the double-sided blackboard.

Session 7

Worksheet D

Colour as fast as possible.

Worksheet E

Initial letter game

Category	Letter:	Letter:	Letter:
Boy's name			
Girl's name			
Colour			
Item of clothing			
Food			
Vegetable			
Animal			
Machine			
Town			
Country			
Musical instrument			
Sport			
Job			
Score			

Session 7

Equipment

Lined A4 paper, carbon-paper message pads, selection of writing instruments

1   Warm-up exercises

○   Begin the session by doing the warm-up exercises.   (10 minutes)

2   Homework review

○   Look at the homework sheets.   (4–5 minutes)

3   Words within words

○   Give each child a sheet of lined A4 paper. Suggest a word with at least 8 letters, for example: encouragement. Ask the children to write this in cursive script at the top of the paper. They then make as many words as they can from that word in 2 minutes, writing the new words underneath, using the writing instrument of their choice. Check the words all together, scoring as follows:

1 point for each correct word

2 points for a correct word not made by anyone else.

○   Play two more rounds, inviting children to suggest the main word.   (10 minutes)

4   101 uses

○   Suggest an everyday object and ask the children to think of some alternative uses for it, writing down in cursive script as many as they can. For example, a pair of spectacles could be used as a magnifying glass, a way of starting a fire or a disguise. Encourage the children to be creative in their thinking. Children could swap sheets for marking, awarding 1 point for each legibly written idea; 2 points for an idea that no one else has thought of.   (10 minutes)

5   Write a letter

○   Ask the children to write a letter in cursive script to someone who is having difficulties with handwriting, suggesting some ideas that may help them.

          (15 minutes)

6   Secret messages

○   Before the session, make up a writing pad for each child consisting of four layers of plain paper with a sheet of carbon paper between. Ask the children to write a 'secret message' on the top sheet of paper. Then get them to check how many of the sheets below the message have been imprinted. The idea is to try to write with just enough pressure to get the message on the second sheet only.

          (10 minutes)

7   Ending the programme

○   At the end of this session, thank the children for all their hard work. Give praise for their efforts and explain that they will each be assessing their handwriting with you (or the teacher or therapist) as they did before the start of the programme in order to see exactly what progress they have made and to discuss how they can continue to develop and improve their skills.

Begin the test with the child standing up straight, arms by their sides and legs together. Their hands should be fisted, with the index finger pointing to the floor. Their eyes should be closed throughout.

Move the child's limbs to the position shown in each diagram and then return them to the starting position. Then ask the child to perform the same movement independently, returning to the start position with eyes still closed. Mark each response by ticking the appropriate column.

Body position	Accurate	Almost accurate	Incorrect
Single movements			
1 Place the right index finger on the left shoulder.			
2 Place the left index finger on the right ear.			
3 Place the right index finger on the tip of the nose.			
4 Place the right index finger on the left elbow.			
5 Place the left index finger on the right knee.			
6 Place the right index finger on the right shoulder.			
7 Place the left index finger on the left eye.			
8 Place both left and right hands on opposite shoulders.			

Test of kinaesthetic acuity

Body position	Accurate	Almost accurate	Incorrect
Sequential movements			
9 Place the right index finger on the nose, then on the left ear, then on the left elbow.			
10 Place the left index finger on the right knee, then on the left knee, then on the nose.			
11 Place the right index finger on the left eye, then on the nose, then on the right shoulder.			
12 Place the left index finger on the right shoulder, then left shoulder, then nose.			
13 Place the right index finger on the left eye, then on the left shoulder, then on the left elbow.			
14 Place the left index finger on the right elbow, then on the right knee, then on the nose.			
15 Place both the left and right index fingers on opposite ears, then on opposite shoulders, then on opposite eyes.			

Addy, L M (1995) An evaluation of a perceptuo-motor approach to handwriting, Unpublished Master's thesis. University of York

Allcock, P (2001) 'The understated difficulties of slow handwriting', *Handwriting Today*, vol. 1, pp. 56–61

Alston, J (1995) *Assessing and Promoting Writing Skills*. NASEN

Ayres, J (1979) *Sensory Integration and the Child*. Los Angeles: Western Psychological Services

Carter, J N and Synolds, D (1974) 'Effects of relaxation training upon handwriting quality', *Journal of Learning Disabilities*, vol. 7, pp. 53–55

Charter, D (2000) 'Poor handwriting can cost a GCSE grade', *The Times*, 5 June 2000, p. 4

Cripps, C (2001) 'Getting it write from the start', Study Day Notes, St John College, York, 28.2.01

Dooijes, E H (1983) 'Analysis of handwriting movements', *Acta Psychologica*, vol. 54, pp. 99–114

Dutton, K P (1992) 'Writing under examination conditions: establishing a baseline', *Handwriting Review*, vol. 7, pp. 80–102

Geddes, D (1981) *Psychomotor Individualised Programs for Intellectual, Learning and Behavioral Disabilities*. Boston: Allyn and Bacon

Graves, D (1980) *Balance the Basics: Let Them Write*. New York: Ford Foundation

Harris, S J and Livesey, D J (1992) 'Improving handwriting through kinaesthetic sensitivity practice', *Australian Occupational Therapy Journal*, vol. 39, pp. 23–27

Kao, H S R (1973) 'Handwriting ergonomics', *Visible Language*, vol. 13 (3), pp. 331–339

Kerr, R (1982) *Psychomotor Learning*. Holt, Rinehart & Winston

Kirshner, A J (1972) *Training that Makes Sense*. Academic Therapy Publications

Laszlo, J I and Bairstow P J (1984) 'Handwriting difficulties and possible solutions', *School Psychology International*, vol. 5, pp. 207–213

Levine, M D, Oberklaid, F and Meltzer, L (1981) 'Developmental output failure: a study of low productivity in school-aged children', *Pediatrics*, vol. 67, pp. 8–25

Mason, R (1991) 'Handwriting following transfer to secondary school – some interim research notes', *Handwriting Review*, pp. 43–48

Roe, M D (1994) 'A rational approach to handwriting models', *Handwriting Review*, pp. 22–34

Schneck, C M (1991) 'Comparison of pencil-grip patterns in first graders with good and poor writing skills', *The American Journal of Occupational Therapy*, vol. 45 (8), pp. 701–706

Sims, K, Henderson, S E, Hulme, C and Morton, J (1996) 'The remediation of clumsiness. II: Is kinesthesis the answer?', *Developmental Medicine and Child Neurology*, vol. 38, pp. 988–997

Summers, J (2001) 'Joint laxity in the index finger and thumb and its relationship to pencil grasps used by children', *Australian Journal of Occupational Therapy*, vol. 48, pp. 132–141

Teasdale, N, Forget, R, Bard, C, Paillard, J, Fleury, M and Lamarre, Y (1993) 'The role of proprioception information for the production of isometric forces and for handwriting tasks', *Acta Psychologica*, vol. 82 (1–3), pp. 179–191

Teodorescu, I and Addy, L (1996) *Write from the Start*, Wisbech: LDA

Verschueren, S M P, Swinnen, S P, Cordo, P J and Dounskaia, N (1999) 'Proprioceptive control of multijoint movement: bimanual circle drawing', *Experimental Brain Research*, vol. 127 (2), pp. 182–192

The following resources may be useful.

Callirobics™ by Liora Laufer
A unique concept in handwriting exercises. They consist of repetitive simple writing patterns (straight and curved lines) to music. The music relaxes the participants and adds rhythm to the exercises. With music the exercises become fun instead of a tedious penmanship chore. Music also benefits participants who learn better through auditory rather than visual means. Available from: PO Box 6634, Charlottesville, VA 22906, USA; tel.: 1-800-769-2891; fax: 1-434-293-9008

Evaluation Tool of Children's Handwriting (1995) by Amundson
Publisher: OT Kids Inc, PO Box 1118, Homer, Alaska 99603, USA; otkids@alaska.net

Handwriting Speed Test (1996) by Wallen, Bonney and Lennox
Available from: Australian Association of Occupational Therapists www.otnsw.com.au

Handwriting without Tears by Jan Olsen
Available from: Psychological Corporation, Harcourt Education, Halley Court, Jordan Hill, Oxford OX2 8EJ

Loops and Other Groups by Mary Benbow
Available from: Psychological Corporation (address as above)

Minnesota Handwriting Assessment (1999) by Judith Reisman
Available from: Psychological Corporation (address as above)

Structured Cursive Writing by Phillips and Leonard
A structured multisensory handwriting programme.
Available from: Ann Arbor Publishers Ltd, PO Box 1, Belford, Northumberland NE70 7JX; www.annarbor.co.uk

Teaching Handwriting: Continuous Cursive Handwriting and How to Teach it (2001) by Henderson, Bodle and Stratton
Available from: The Beacon Office, Oldfield School, Chiltern Road, Maidenhead, Berkshire SL6 1XA; tel.: 01628 675876
oldfieldbeacon@btinternet.com

Victorian modern cursive script
Downloadable electronic fonts available at:
www.sofweb.vic.edu.au/eys/resources/handwriting.htm

Write Dance by Ragnhild Oussoren Voors
Publisher: Lucky Duck Publishing Ltd, 3 Thorndale Mews, Clifton, Bristol BS8 2HX
tel.: 0117 9732881
www.luckyduck.co.uk